The CANADIAN FLOWER ARRANGER

The Garden Clubs of Ontario

Photography TIM SAUNDERS

Writer HELEN SKINNER

Creative Director PEG SPENCE

Project Co-ordinator SUZANNE DRINKWATER

Flower Arrangements MEMBERS OF THE GARDEN CLUBS OF ONTARIO

Macmillan Canada

Canadian Cataloguing in Publication Data

Main entry under title:

The Canadian flower arranger

Includes index.
ISBN 0-7715-9188-8

1. Flower arrangement–Canada.   I. Garden Clubs of Ontario.

SB449.C36 1993   745.92'0971   C92-095502-9

Production Coordinator: Janice Brett

Printed in Hong Kong
by Book Art Inc., Toronto, for
Macmillan Canada
A Division of Canada Publishing Corporation
Toronto, Canada

1 2 3 4 5   97 96 95 94 93

TO ALL FLOWER ARRANGERS

$\mathcal{A}$CKNOWLEDGEMENTS

The Garden Clubs of Ontario gratefully acknowledges the help of individual club members and interested friends who gave unstintingly of their time, creative talents, and expertise. An entire book would not be big enough to include all their names, but in particular we thank Mary Baillie, Marisa Bergagnini, Shirley Binns, Lotte Brunner, Lynn Cantor, Shirley Crang, Joan Creighton, Joyce Dietrich, Betty Ewens, Colomba Fuller, Beth Frost, Susan Gibson, DeeDee Gracey, Trudy Grantham, Lillie Haworth, Doreen Henry, Yvonne Hubbs, Barbara Ann Hynes, Ella Irving, Robbie Isbister, Marie Kennedy, Mary Kernohan, Teresa Kubilis, Marian Lawson, Georgie Lefroy, Dora W. MacKay, Margaret Marcar, Anne McLeod, Joan McMullen, Audrey Meiklejohn, Georgina Mentis, Mary Anne Miller, Betty Peebles, Beth Porter, Charlotte Smith, Mary van Straubenzee, Dodie Wesley, Pearl Wilby; from the Civic Garden Centre Library and Bookshop, Mavis Griffin, Pamela MacKenzie, Barbara Stevenson, and from the Royal Botanical Gardens, the Director Allen Paterson.

The Canadian Flower Arranger book committee:
Debbie Beattie, Suzanne Drinkwater, Heather Fuller, Beverly Hargraft, Doreen Martindale, Helen Skinner, and Peg Spence.
Ex officio: Ann Diebel, Katie May McCarthy.

Contents

$\mathscr{I}$NTRODUCTION

The art of designing with flowers has its origins in antiquity. It can be seen in Egyptian tomb paintings, in Roman mosaics and on Grecian urns. Paintings, from the Reformation to the present, record a continual interest in the artful placement of flowers in containers, in a fascinating variety of forms and styles. But pictures are only likenesses. A fresh flower arrangement, while as ephemeral as the sound of a symphonic variation, can capture movement, colour, and imagination in an exquisite evocation of creation.

Floral art in Canada has had many influences. Pioneers to this country were introduced to flowers of the new world by native peoples, who taught them about plants that could be used as food and others that were useful in medicines. It was not long before many of the new flowers were gathered simply to brighten log cabins. In 1830 one settler wrote that when she went to the swamp she gathered some branches of cedar to form the background for a flower pot, the front of which was to be filled with white pearly everlastings.

Through the years, while Canadians continued to design with flowers, many from their own gardens, they saw in books, magazines, and art, the development of flower arranging styles all over the world. For two centuries European flower paintings set a fashion for brilliant bouquets filled with a wonderful variety of flowers. From the United States came different trends. As well as traditional designs, emphasis was placed on line—a curving branch, an upright stem, and form—an individual flower or a small grouping of flowers. A clean, sparse look was advocated. At present a sculptural effect, achieved by a disciplined control of foliage and flowers, is appearing in floral designs from France and Italy.

Japan, too, has had an effect on many aspects of international floral art. *Ikebana,* the Japanese art of flower arranging, teaches discipline, appreciation of each component, and an understanding of the delicate relationship between humans and their living environment.

All these influences have been seen in Canadian flower shows, where designers have adopted and adapted much from abroad. Yet there is a difference. Floral art in Canada owes its style to many cultures, but an individuality has come from the land, the land that the pioneers sought. Just as the land and its surrounding waters are in Canada's music, sculpture, and paintings, so also can they be seen in its floral designs, where frequently a more naturalistic feeling dominates the placement of flowers, foliage, driftwood, and rocks.

A Canadian "style" in floral design, however, is impossible to define. As with all art forms, floral art is constantly changing. Patterns from other cultures are absorbed, new ideas appear, and the designer's innate creativity is woven into the art piece. This first book on Canadian floral art does not define a Canadian style, but it does illustrate the wonderful variety of designs from Canadian arrangers.

TIME MAKES A GARDEN

Shirley Binns

THE DESIGN	Creative−Vegetative, all foliage
INSIGHT	The green garden of a nearby marsh has been growing for centuries. It has hundreds of plants in a variety of shades, colours, forms and heights, and an equal number of creatures that keep it swirling and humming with life.
MATERIALS	Artemesia *Artemesia ludoviciana var. albula* 'Silver King' Bamboo, locally gathered, probably *Arundinaria japonica* Red Barberry *Berberis atropurpurea* Cattail reeds *Typha latifolia* Golden Euonymus *Euonymus fortunei* 'Sheridan Gold' Hosta *Hosta aureo marginata & H.plantaginea* Iris leaves *Iris germanica* Sedum, variegated *Sedum spectabile* 'Variegatum' Solomon's seal *Polygonatum biflorum* Cedar tree root *Thuja occidentalis*
METHOD	*The container is shaped irregularly, rather like a leaf* *from which a bug has taken a bite or three. Three holders are used.* *A pincup, raised by a brown, floral tape-covered tin and set* *outside the container in one of the bites, holds the tallest materials.* *To the left, a pinholder in the container holds those of medium* *height, and to the right, another holds the iris foliage.*

Spirit of Fall

Audrey Meiklejohn

THE DESIGN   Creative–Free style

INSIGHT   Autumn in Canada brings an exuberance of colour.
Turning leaves and flowers mix and blur the landscape
with a kaleidescope of crimson, orange, gold, and blue.
Just a few leaves and flowers, held in place, can capture the
season with each hue and shade distinct and clear.

MATERIALS   Chrysanthemum *Chrysanthemum* 'Statesman'

Dahlia hybrid *Dahlia* 'Davenport Lesley'

Sugar Maple leaves *Acer saccharum*

Lacquered Bamboo

METHOD   *The maple leaves are pruned so that they balance*
in the bamboo opening and two narrow tumblers
inside the bamboo stalks hold water for the flowers.

SPRING

Lillie Haworth

THE DESIGN   Traditional Line—Mass

INSIGHT   Spring comes slowly at first to much of Canada
with the yellowing of willows, the fuzz of pussywillow
buds, the gradual appearance of colour on forsythia
branches. Then it explodes like a sunburst with
brilliant yellow daffodils.

MATERIALS   Daffodil *Narcissus cv.*

Forsythia *Forsythia x intermedia cv.*

Pussy Willow *Salix discolor*

Geranium leaves *Pelargonium zonale cv.*

Antique bottle

METHOD   *A Mayfair cup filled with a piece of oasis is secured*
to the top of the bottle with stickum. It is completely
hidden by flowers and geranium leaves. Rhythm is achieved
both by the flowing line and by flowers in different stages
of development, from buds at the outer edges of the design
to full-blown flowers at the centre.

SIMPLICITY

Peg Spence

THE DESIGN Creative–Parallel

INSIGHT A modern painting by Canadian artist Ray Cattall
has bright colour and clear spaces.

MATERIALS Miniature Agapanthus *Agapanthus africanus nanus*
Gayfeather *Liatris spicata*
Columbine *Aquilegia vulgaris*
Daisy Chrysanthemum *Chrysanthemum* 'Casa'
Euonymus *Euonymus fortunei* 'Sheridan Gold'
Freesia *Freesia x hybrida*
Iris *Iris siberica*
Lady's Mantle leaves *Alchemilla vulgaris*
Miniature Roses *Rosa cv.*
Snapdragons *Antirrhinum majus*
Bergenia leaves *Bergenia cordifolia*
Plastic tray filled with moss-covered oasis

METHOD *A parallel design has three or more vertical
groupings of materials. The space between the lines
is important in defining the parallel effect.*

CASTLE IN THE AIR

Joyce Dietrich

THE DESIGN   Creative–Interpretive

INSIGHT   A castle in the air was first seen at Laurel Creek near Kitchener. Wisps of marsh mist cluster around silvery tree roots catching the light and create, in an instant, a vision of legendary castle towers, knights of old, and Merlin's mystic spells.

MATERIALS   Baby's breath *Gypsophila paniculata*

Statice *Limonium sinuatum*

Pampas Grass, *Cortaderia selloana*

Driftwood

METHOD   *Thin pieces of bamboo are attached to and support a metal wreath form. This holds the wet oasis into which the pampas grass, pink and yellow statice, and baby's breath are placed.*

FIGURE EIGHT

Beth Porter

THE DESIGN   Miniature; Creative–Free style

INSIGHT   Sweeping curves and rounded figures on clean ice
are the trails left by practising skaters.

MATERIALS   Queen Anne's Lace *Daucus carota*

Beargrass *Xerophyllum tenax*

METHOD   *Beargrass is an ideal plant for miniature*
arrangements. It is wide enough to give substance,
narrow enough to be in scale, soft enough when
upright to look natural, and pliable enough to form
curves and circles without breaking. Queen Anne's Lace,
too, is useful. Separated flower umbels are perfectly
in scale for a design that is less than five inches.

$\mathcal{S}$YNERGISM

Georgina Mentis

THE DESIGN   Creative–Synergistic

INSIGHT   Nautilus shells, with their high-gloss satin finish have the loops and swirls of a roller coaster.

MATERIALS   Pink Astilbe *Astilbe cv.*

Climbing Rose *Rosa* 'Swan Lake'

Cane

Nautilus shells

METHOD   *Synergistic designs are composed of three or more similar arrangements and placed so that they become one design. Here, three acrylic rods hold the individual designs. Loops of cane and the repetition of the shells and flowers in the arrangement unify the whole.*

SUNBURST

Robbie Isbister

THE DESIGN   Creative–Free style

INSIGHT   An olive green Japanese ceramic container makes
an unobtrusive foil for bright colour. Its glazed diagonal
stripes carry the design line right to the base.

MATERIALS   Daisy Chrysanthemum *Chrysanthemum* 'White Refla'

Cream Lilies *Lilium* 'Sterling Silver'

Branches of Weeping Mulberry *Moraceae pendula*

METHOD   *The container is weighted with small
stones two-thirds of the way up which gives
it a firm surface for the pinholder.*

SHAPE OF THINGS TO COME

Beth Frost

THE DESIGN   Creative–Interpretive

INSIGHT   Old-fashioned peonies are just coming into bloom
and the flower show title is "The shape of things to come."
Fashions in design may be old or futuristic; fortunately,
peonies are past, present, and future.

MATERIALS   Lady's Mantle *Alchemilla vulgaris*

Garden Peonies *Paeonia cv.*

Hosta *Hosta sieboldiana* 'Elegans'

Iris leaves *Iris pseudacorus*

METHOD   *Peonies can last for three weeks. If picked
when the buds are soft with just a hint of colour,
wrapped in plastic, and kept in the refrigerator
(out of water), when they are taken out and conditioned
for 48 hours they open as if new. A sturdy wrought
iron stand composed of three pieces, for ease of
carrying, is invaluable. It is plain and simple
and appropriate for any arrangement.*

$\mathcal{A}$PPROACHING WINTER

Mary Baillie

THE DESIGN   Creative–Free style

INSIGHT   Winds move through leaves and berries at the edge
of the wood; shafts of sunlight catch their colours against
the crisp, clear blue of the sky. It is autumn.

MATERIALS   Cherry branches *Prunus* 'Printemps'

Rose hips *Rosa multiflora*

Yellow lilies *Lilium* 'Medallion'

METHOD   *Two-thirds of the container is filled
with pebbles to provide a balancing weight.
The pinholder sits on the pebbles.*

Study in Contrast
Teresa Kubilis

THE DESIGN   Creative–Free style

INSIGHT   Contrasts are in surfaces, smooth or fuzzy;
in sizes, large or small; in colours, brilliant
or dull; and in lines, straight or curved.

MATERIALS   Tulip *Tulipa cv.*

Asparagus fern *Asparagus setaceus* 'Plumosus'

Corn plant foliage *Zea mays*

Iris leaves *Iris cv.*

METHOD   *The handcrafted container consists of five pieces glued
together with water-soluble glue. At the top a spray paint
can cover conceals a pinholder; then a tin, open at both
ends, is glued to a glass bottle weighted with pebbles or
sand, which has two small plastic vials fixed at the back
at different levels. The whole is undercoated with flat
paint or glue to make a surface on which, when dry, a finish
of polyfilla and glue (mixed to a spreadable consistency)
is generously painted to create the desired shape.
The completed container is then painted with a semi-gloss
or eggshell finish and antiqued with black shoe polish.*

CHRISTMAS PARTY

Marian Lawson

THE DESIGN   Traditional–Mass

INSIGHT   Christmas parties make the house warm and cheerful,
countering the chill effect of ice and snow outdoors.
Christmas flowers reflect both the temperature contrast
in colour, warmth, and gaiety and, with their overflowing
generosity, the spirit of the season.

MATERIALS   Alstroemeria *Alstroemeria* 'Rosita'
Carnation *Dianthus* 'Astor'
Gerbera *Gerbera* 'Pascal'
Gladiolus *Gladiolus* 'Hunting song'
Mountain Ash berries *Sorbus aucuparia*
Poinsettia *Euphorbia pulcherrima*
Roses *Rosa* 'Sonia'
Eucalyptus *Eucalyptus perriniana*
Ivy *Hedera helix* 'Baltica'
Japanese Spurge *Pachysandra terminalis*
Spruce *Picea glauca*
White Pine *Pinus strobus*

METHOD   *Making a flower arrangement in front of a window
presents a particular problem. Light penetrating
the arrangement spoils the desired effect unless there
is a solid base of foliage before the flowers are added.*

*F*ALL FARE

Marie Kennedy

THE DESIGN   Creative–Modern Mass

INSIGHT   Ornamental Kale and its multiples of crisp, clean leaves epitomizes the bountiful harvest. All the other fruit and vegetables reinforce the fact that this is a delicious time to fill the root cellar with baskets of fall fare.

MATERIALS   Apple *Malus pumila cv.*
Broccoli *Brassica olearacea botrytis*
Grapes *Vitis cv.*
Ornamental Kale *Brassica oleracea acephala* 'White Peacock'
Peppers *Capsicum annuum*
Bittersweet *Celastrus scandens*
Wheat *Triticum aestivum*

METHOD   *Filling a basket with vegetables, fruit,*
and flowers to give a feeling of abundance is easy
using wired fruitsticks and flower waterpicks,
but arranging wheat and bittersweet to achieve
a desired direction on the handle presents
a problem which is solved by hot glue applied
with a glue gun.

RACING WITH THE MOON

Ella Irving

THE DESIGN   Creative—Free style

INSIGHT   Light through the spaces of the dark, modern Japanese container glows like the moon in the night sky.

MATERIALS   Banana leaves *Musa paradisiaca*

Ginger *Zingiber officinale*

Lotus pods *Nelumbo lutea*

Wisteria vine *Wisteria floribunda*

METHOD   *The very small opening of the container necessitates bunching the materials tightly enough that they will stay in place without any mechanical device.*

CORAL MADNESS

Anne McLeod

THE DESIGN	Traditional–Mass
INSIGHT	Two of the plants commemorating Toronto are a beautiful coral colour. The tulip is named for the city and the rose for a citizen.
MATERIALS	Chrysanthemum, single *Chrysanthemum* 'Casa' Delphinium *Delphinium cv.* Queen Anne's Lace *Daucus carota* Rose *Rosa* 'Sonia' Tulip *Tulipa* 'Toronto' Boston Fern *Nephrolepis exaltata var. bostoniensis* Elderberry *Sambucus canadensis* Geranium *Pelargonium cv.*
METHOD	*Delicate Queen Anne's Lace and green Elderberry branches outline the design and carry the green and white colours to the centre, to white chrysanthemums and foliage. Open coral flowers bring weight to the centre of the design and a blue delphinium draws the eye into the third dimension.*

AYSIDE

Dodie Wesley

THE DESIGN   Traditional–Line-Mass

INSIGHT   A walk along the cottage road is meandering
and slow, because one is frequently distracted
by the colours and textures of "weeds" in the
ditches and shoulders.

MATERIALS   Cattail *Typha augustifolia*
Dock *Rumex crispus*
Lily *Lilium* 'Le Reve'
Loosestrife *Lythrum salicaria*
Spurge, flowering *Euphorbia corollata*
Soft Rush *Juncus effusus*
Yarrow *Achillea millefolium*
Hosta *Hosta cv.*

METHOD   *Cattails and dock are excellent line material.*
Their stalks stay straight and firm as the mass
of the design is filled in around and beside them.
As the rushes dry, they curl a little, adding
softness and grace to the line.

$\mathcal{P}$ETIT POINT

Pearl Wilby

THE DESIGN   Small Design; Traditional–Asymmetric Mass

INSIGHT   The garden has many plants with little flowers both colourful and short-stemmed. They are perfect for a design that is not much larger than a delphinium floret.

MATERIALS   Campanula *Campanula muralis* 'Portenschlagiana'

Delphinium floret *Delphinium cv.*

Lady's Mantle *Alchemilla vulgaris*

Salvia *Salvia farinacea*

Miniature euonymus *Euonymus fortunei* 'Kewensis' 'Minima'

METHOD   *Small designs are technically easier than miniatures because the flower stems are usually long and strong enough to be put into oasis with fingers instead of tweezers. However, good proportion and the proper scale are harder to achieve with small designs.*

COMBINATION

Yvonne Hubbs

THE DESIGN   Traditional–Mass, Fruit and Vegetable

INSIGHT   Fruit and vegetable designs are often dictated by the
seasons. In winter and spring they may be sparse and modern,
then bountiful in summer and fall. Late September harvests
bring masses of vegetables, fruit, foliage, and flowers,
and wonderful russet, green, and gold colours.

MATERIALS   Apples *Malus cv.*
Brussels Sprouts *Brassica oleracea var. gemmifera*
Chrysanthemums *Chrysanthemum cv.*
Gladiolus *Gladiolus cv.*
Miniature Pumpkins *Cucurbita* 'Autumn Gold'
Ornamental Kale *Brassica oleracea acephala*
Sweet Peppers *Capsicum annuum*
Sweet Potato Squash *Cucurbita maxima* 'Delicata'
Beargrass *Xerophyllum tenax*
Euonymus *Euonymus fortunei* 'Variegata'
Ivy *Hedera helix*
Grapes *Vitis sp.*

METHOD   *A broom handle is cemented into a juice tin. This is placed in an oasis-filled
container, which is then covered with chicken wire. Close to the top of the broom-
stick is wired another piece of oasis covered in chicken wire. Wooden skewers,
wired to or inserted in the fruit and vegetables, hold them firmly in the oasis.*

Woodland Awakening

Doreen Henry

THE DESIGN   Creative–Interpretive, featuring decorative wood

INSIGHT   A piece of driftwood comes to life, like a creature, from the leaves and wood on the forest floor.

MATERIALS   Iris *Iris* 'Yellow Gleam'

Contorted Willow *Salix matsudana* 'Tortuosa'

Mugho Pine *Pinus* 'Mugo'

Fungus *Ganoderma applanatum*

Slate

METHOD   *A lead base with centre screw attached holds the wood upright. Flowers and branches are in a pincup behind the wood.*

$\mathcal{I}$NSPIRATION

Georgie Lefroy

THE DESIGN   Creative–Interpretive

INSIGHT   The art of Benjamin Chee Chee captures movement in swift flowing lines. Grapevine, which winds through tree branches during the growing season, is the "line" for this flower show class title: "Inspired by Art of the Native Peoples of Canada."

MATERIALS   Bittersweet *Celastrus scandens*

Oak leaves *Quercus sp.*

Grapevine *Vitis labrusca*

Oak burl *Quercus sp.*

Bricks

METHOD   *Bricks, blackened with shoe polish and spray paint, form a heavy base to hold the weight of oak burl and grapevine, also blackened, and hide the pincups holding the flowers.*

$\mathcal{F}$LOWERS IN CLAY

Marie Kennedy

THE DESIGN   Creative–Modern Line-Mass

INSIGHT   Spring flowers push their way up through last year's vines, old leaves, and fungus to bring new life and colour to a brown, dry landscape.

MATERIALS   Daffodil *Narcissus cv.*
Grape Hyacinth *Muscari sp.*
Hens and Chickens *Sempervivum sobaliferum*
Hyacinth *Hyacinthus cv.*
Iris *Iris cv.*
Kalanchoe *Kalanchoe cv.*
Tulip *Tulipa* 'Queen of Bartigons'
Elk fern *Nephrolepis cv.*
Galax *Galax aphylla*
Wild Grape Vine *Vitis riparia*
Artist's Fungus *Ganoderma applanatum*
Heavy Clay pot

METHOD   *The flowers are grouped and "terraced"*
(in a step-like fashion) to give strong colour
and to balance the clay pot.

LINES AND ROUNDS

Mary Baillie

THE DESIGN   Creative–Abstract

INSIGHT   When a large sumac tree is felled and split, the
                 heartwood reveals surprising dark lines and lighter ones,
                 which catch the light.

MATERIALS   Rose *Rosa* 'Matangi'

                 Golden Privet leaves *Ligustrum vicaryi* 'Aureum'

                 Smoke bush *Cotinus coggygria*

                 Sumac wood *Rhus typhina*

METHOD   *The materials are placed in different spaces*
                 to give balance and stability. Double-sided tape
                 holds the rounds in place, and a small funnel
                 with extender holds the rose.

$\mathcal{A}$ Basket for Mother's Day

Shirley Crang

THE DESIGN   Traditional–Mass

INSIGHT   For this Mother's Day the flowers are the message— ivy for longevity, daisies for integrity, chrysanthemums for spice, and roses for love.

MATERIALS   White Aster *Aster ericoides* 'Monte casino'

White Chrysanthemum, single *Chrysanthemum* 'Casa'

White Rose *Rosa* 'Jack Frost'

Living Ivy basket *Hedera helix*

METHOD   *For the ivy basket, a wire basket is padded with wet sphagnum moss. Short cuttings of ivy, the smaller the leaf the better (hedera helix 'Needlepoint,' for example) are inserted into the sphagnum. Long pieces, also inserted, are then intertwined over the handle. The basket is kept moist and, as the cuttings take root and grow, they are twisted through, wound over and under, and pruned until the basket is evenly covered. Growing time is about one year.*

Sunny Days

Katie May McCarthy

THE DESIGN   Traditional—Mass

INSIGHT   Cottage guests arriving by boat are welcomed
by a basket of country flowers on the dock.

MATERIALS   Astilbe *Astilbe cv.*
Foxglove *Digitalis purpurea*
Hawkweed *Hieracium canadense*
Jacob's Ladder *Polemonium caeruleum*
Meadowrue *Thalictrum polygamum*
Lady's Mantle *Alchemilla vulgaris*
Loosestrife *Lythrum salicaria*
Queen Anne's Lace *Daucus carota*
Shasta Daisy *Chrysanthemum maximum cv.*
Sweet Clover *Melilotus alba*
Veronica *Veronica spicata*
Cedar, red *Juniperus virginianus*
Huckleberry leaves *Gaylussacia baccata*
Hosta *Hosta cv.*
White Pine *Pinus strobus*

METHOD   *White predominates and is made more intense
by the addition of small blue, pink, and yellow flowers.*

MEMORIES

Dora W. MacKay

THE DESIGN   Traditional–Mass

INSIGHT   Over the years an avid gardener collects plants.
Some are gifts, some commemorate special occasions,
and some are "found." Most have a history,
and whenever the plants are cultivated or cut their
stories are remembered.

MATERIALS   Clematis *Clematis cv.*
Columbine *Aquilegia cv.*
Coral Bell *Heuchera sanguinea* 'Splendens'
Lady's Mantle *Alchemilla vulgaris*
Lavender *Lavandula officinalis*
Meadow Rue *Thalictrum adiantifolium*
Physostegia *Physostegia virginana* 'Summer Glow'
Roses *Rosa* 'Electron,' 'Lancome,' 'Sexy Rexy'
Veronica *Veronica latifolia*
Variegated Euonymus *Euonymus fortunei* 'Emerald Gaiety'

METHOD   *Garden flowers that are well conditioned
have stems that are firm or turgid with water.
As a result they push into oasis easily,
a most important factor in the construction
of a free-standing design.*

SPRING THAW

Marisa Bergagnini

THE DESIGN   Traditional—Line, Water viewing

INSIGHT   Crimson, fluffy florettes tip the branches of the
Sugar Maple. One young tree arching over the river bank
has its roots in the swollen, icy waters of the spring thaw
while, in a quiet backwater, the buds of native iris,
I. versicolour, are showing blue.

MATERIALS   Maple *Acer saccharum*

Iris *Iris xiphium* 'Blue Magic'

Begonia leaves *Begonia mellon*

METHOD   *A pinholder hidden by begonia leaves holds branches
and flowers. Clear water, a major component of a water
viewing arrangement, is added when the container
is free of plant debris and/or soil.*

UNE

Peg Spence

THE DESIGN   Traditional–Mass

INSIGHT   The single red peony, *Paeonia* 'Cythera'

MATERIALS   Alstroemeria *Alstroemeria* 'Jumbo'
Clematis *Clematis x Jackmanii*
Cornflower *Centaurea cyanus*
Delphinium *Delphinium cv.*
Deutzia *Deutzia gracilis*
Lady's Mantle *Alchemilla vulgaris*
Peony *Paeonia* 'Cythera'
Poppy *Papaver nudicaule*
Weigela *Weigela florida* 'Variegata'
Black porcelain urn

METHOD   *The outline for this traditional triangular*
mass is formed with alstroemeria and weigela.
Flower shapes and colours are chosen to give
a varied yet unified background to the peonies.

WELCOME

Margaret Marcar

THE DESIGN   Creative—Underwater (Modern Mass)

INSIGHT   Marble top and mirror have a sophistication that should
be complemented with a modern outline and clear colour.

MATERIALS   Lily *Lilium* 'Matchless'

Lisianthus *Eustoma grandiflorum*

Galax *Galax aphylla*

Hosta *Hosta cv.*

Corkscrew Willow *Salix matsudana* 'Tortuosa'

METHOD   *Corkscrew willow is held in place in the water
by a piece of oasis wedged into the top of the
container and extending three fingers above it.
(Underwater components are also part of the design.)
More willow and flowers are placed at the top
of the oasis.*

COUNTRY WEDDING

Trudy Grantham

THE DESIGN	Creative–Modern Mass
INSIGHT	An old iron pot from a country kitchen, roses and lilies celebrate a fall wedding.
MATERIALS	Lily *Lilium* 'Sterling Star' Love-Lies-Bleeding *Amaranthus caudatus* Pepper *Capsicum annuum* Rose *Rosa maitaranga* 'Marela' Bittersweet *Celastrus scandens* Camellia leaves *Camellia japonica* Ivy *Hedera helix* Rosehips *Rosa multiflora*
METHOD	*Roses set the mood at a wedding. Yet to give the design interest and rhythm the supplementary materials must be placed so that each element's distinct quality is displayed as the colours are carried through the arrangement.*

Cottage Country

Mary Kernohan

THE DESIGN   Creative–Interpretive, featuring wood

INSIGHT   Roadside lilies, escapees from early settler's gardens, grow like wildflowers along country roads, frequently smothering the remains of original root fences.

MATERIALS   Day Lilies *Hemerocallis fulva*

Sumac *Rhus typhina*

Driftwood

METHOD   *Driftwood, washed up on the shores of Lake Huron often has beautiful shapes and surface striations. Brushing, cleaning, and a little sanding bring out the highlights.*

*O*CTOBERFEST

Barbara Ann Hynes

THE DESIGN   Creative—Wall hanging

INSIGHT   "Purple and fine linen" indicate a feast fit for a king.
A door hanging may prepare guests for just such a party.

MATERIALS   Grapes *Vitis labrusca* 'Concord'

Ornamental Kale *Brassica oleracea acephela*

Pear *Pyrus communis cv.*

Ivy *Hedera helix*

Virginia Creeper *Parthenocissus quinquefolia*

METHOD   *An oasis cage with a flat back holds kale,*
ivy, and wired fruit and, with its own hook,
hangs easily on the door.

SPRING FLING

Anne McLeod

THE DESIGN	Traditional–Mass
INSIGHT	Spring growth is light and airy. Through leafing and flowering branches the sky is easily seen. Spring's colour is yellow.
MATERIALS	Daffodil *Narcissus cv.*
	Delphinium *Delphinium cv.*
	Forsythia *Forsythia x intermedia cv.*
	Solidaster *Solidaster luteus*
	Parrot tulip *Tulipa gesnerana* 'Dracontia'
	Yellow and red single tulip *Tulipa cv.*
	Salal *Gaultheria shallon*
	Tole urn
METHOD	*A loose outline of forsythia is repeated with partially open tulips and daffodils. Fully open flowers bring interest to the centre of the design, while blue delphinium gives it depth.*

On the Sunny Side
Margaret Marcar

THE DESIGN   Creative—Free style

INSIGHT   The monochromatic effect of the table and the signed reproduction of Salvador Dali's *Judgement of Paris* above is brightened, both literally and figuratively, by colour and light from the flowers.

MATERIALS   Agapanthus, small flowered *Agapanthus africanus nanus*

Gladiolus *Gladiolus cv.*

Lily *Lilium* 'Medallion'

Galax *Galax aphylla*

New Zealand flax *Phormium tenax* 'Variegatum'

Schefflera *Brassaia actinophylla*

METHOD   *Oasis covered with chicken wire fills a Mayfair cup, which is fixed on top of an acrylic holder.*

*T*HANKSGIVING

Ann Diebel

THE DESIGN   Traditional–Wreath

INSIGHT   The second Monday in October is a time to celebrate the harvest, clear, crisp days, and family and friends coming to the house for a Canadian Thanksgiving.

MATERIALS   Baby's breath *Gypsophila* 'Snow White'

Chrysanthemum *Chrysanthemum* 'Dramatic'

Lily *Lilium* 'Matchless'

Cotoneaster *Cotoneaster cv.*

Ivy *Hedera helix*

METHOD   *Flowers are inserted into an oasis wreath form; a wire hook is fixed to the back and, when hung over a sink for an hour or two, the wreath will be drip-free on the door.*

$\mathcal{P}$RELUDE TO SUMMER

Colomba Fuller

THE DESIGN   Traditional–Mass

INSIGHT   An early summer dinner party has flowers of fresh appeal and gentle fragrance, arranged in an eighteenth-century ormolu compotier low enough for cross-table conversation.

MATERIALS   White Bleeding Heart *Dicentra spectabilis* 'Alba'

Lisianthus *Eustoma grandiflorum*

Peony *Paeonia cv.*

Yellow Rose *Rosa hugonis*

METHOD   *The all-round mass has no major focal point.*
Each visible angle shows flowers and foliage outlining
a low, rounded form with smaller flowers of a deeper
colour providing depth and interest.

$\mathcal{I}$NNOVATION

Mary Baillie

THE DESIGN	Creative–Interpretive
INSIGHT	Stark outlines, spare colours, rocks, and sky resembling the work of Canadian landscape artist, Lawren Harris, are for a flower show competitive class: "Inspired by Art of the Group of Seven."
MATERIALS	Japanese Anemone *Anemone japonica* 'Honorine Jobert' Weathered Juniper branch from Georgian Bay *Juniperus sp.* Pieces of slate from the Humber River
METHOD	*The slate and branch are balanced in front of and hide a heavy metal pincup, which holds the flowers.*

BEYOND THE WINDOW

Betty Peebles

THE DESIGN   Traditional–Line, with accessory

INSIGHT   One of the more tranquil of spring excitements is watching
the buds of the magnolia tree slowly swell, show colour
and then, one by one, gradually open into bloom.

MATERIALS   Magnolia branch *Magnolia x soulangiana*

Tulip *Tulipa* 'Gander's Rhapsody'

Rabbit's-foot fern *Davallia fejeensis*

Amethyst from the region of Thunder Bay

METHOD   *A crescent-shaped pincup placed on the upper*
of two wooden bases is hidden by amethyst and leaves.
The magnolia was cut in late March. Branches were
kept in a pail of warm water and covered with
plastic in the basement. They were sprayed with
room-temperature water daily. Blooms appeared
in twelve days.

DOUBLE DELIGHT

Lotte Brunner

THE DESIGN   Creative–Modern Line-Mass

INSIGHT   The red "wings" of rosa omeiensis Pteracantha thorns are
translucent, the pink roses very fragrant–double delights.

MATERIALS   Coral Bell Foliage *Heuchera sanguinea* 'Splendens'

Roses: *Rosa omeiensis* 'Pteracantha'; *R. rosarium* 'Uetersen'

Smoke Bush *Cotinus coggygria*

METHOD   *The new "iglu" containers of oasis make*
arranging on tall thin stands easier than ever.

$\mathcal{L}$ILAC TIME

Susan Gibson

THE DESIGN   Traditional–Mass

INSIGHT   A sunny morning in the June garden when the last lilac is
in bloom. Peonies are just breaking. The pale pink climbing
rose, New Dawn, is opening on the fence, and purple, pink,
and white self-sown Sweet Rocket is everywhere.

MATERIALS   Lilac *Syringa cv.*
Lily *Lilium* 'Star Gazer'
Lisianthus *Eustoma grandiflorum*
Peony *Paeonia cv.*
Rose *Rosa* 'Sonia'
Stock *Matthiola cv.*
Sweet Rocket *Hesperis matronalis*
Silverleaf Dogwood *Cornus alba* 'Elegantissima'
Venetian glass compote

METHOD   *Dogwood branches provide the points*
for the isosceles triangle outline. Sweet rocket
fills in the lines; deep-coloured lilac gives depth;
peonies and lilies form the major focus; while
small roses, lisianthus, and stocks are variations
on the original theme.

THE FLOWER ARRANGER'S GARDEN

The garden is the most natural source of materials for the flower arranger's art, not only for the flowers themselves but also for the extras: branches, rocks, berries, mosses, fungus, and even an abandoned bird's nest or two. This is not surprising in the growing season but, amazingly enough, a Canadian garden can be quite productive in winter too. Planted with evergreens, shrubs, and trees with interesting stems and vines that twist and twine, the garden has much to offer despite the weather.

Of course, there can be no perfect flower arranger's garden, just as no garden is ever completely perfect for a gardener. For neither one is the art static. However, arrangers and gardeners both use plants which will not only add interest to the garden but will also have the potential of being appropriate for a flower arrangement.

Not only are gardening and flower arranging complementary; they are also nearly synonymous. The trees and shrubs that are the frameworkof a garden frequently provide the height and the line, or the framework, of a flower arrangement. The flowers, the colours and shapes of which are the focal points of the garden, are the focus of most arrangements. With just a little consultation between the two, a nearly perfect flower arranger's garden will be nearly perfect, with just a few additions, for a gardener.

To start with the framework, the trees and shrubs of a flower arranger's garden, the choice will certainly include evergreens. There is variety in the line and depth of conifer branches, length of needles, and size of cones. Each aspect is useful to flower and garden designs, especially in winter. If the garden is large enough, native pine and spruce are handsome, and pine is wonderfully soft to handle. Hemlock, too, adds variety and is a good slow grower for a city lot. Juniper and cedar each have special attributes, and false cypress, another slow grower, has interestingly pendulous tips. Deep, dark yew is easy on the hands when wreaths are being made, and its red berries add a Christmas colour.

Broadleaf evergreens are a heartwarming reminder of summer in the winter garden and their rosettes of leaves are a mainstay in arrangements year round. Not many city arrangers in Canada have large enough rhododendrons to spare branches for cutting, but the faster-growing euonymus, fortunately, needs constant trimming. The variegated green and gold, and gold and white varieties are particularly attractive.

The garden of Robert and Colomba Fuller

There are now hollies that are hardy in Canada, so it is possible to have shiny green holly leaves in flower arrangements, as well as the equally prickly holly-shaped leaves of the long-familiar Oregon grape, mahonia, which for winter arrangements add a warm brown colour.

Native maples, oak and beech branches are often too high for handheld clippers, but their seedlings are easily reached. Mature white birch trees frequently drop useful strips of bark and, if not, flower arrangers' birches get regular prunings. Horse chestnuts are huge trees at maturity, but in one arranger's garden a squirrel-planted chestnut is kept shrub size because the branches, with their soft, downy green-grey buds, are cut annually for spring arrangements.

Willow is one of the arranger's favourite trees, with its pliable young, yellowy branches, but it takes much room and a great deal of water. Less space is taken by the columnar corkscrew willow, whose twisty branches are equally interesting. The Japanese fantail willow has flattened double stems, which are enthusiastically sought for modern arrangements. As for the pussy willow, it too needs plenty of moisture but perhaps the childhood reminiscences it brings are worth the extra watering.

More practical in the flower arranger's garden, especially one in the city, are small trees and shrubs, particularly those that can be forced into bloom ahead of schedule. Two Asian witch hazels, the yellow and the hard-to-find red are excellent for this purpose. Dogwoods, particularly red osier, the Cornelian cherry with its buttons of yellow flowers, the angular yellow twig dogwood for modern arrangements, and, of course, the indispensable forsythias, are all easily grown shrubs that force well and are perfect for spring arrangements.

The flowering fruits, quince, crabapple, and cherry can also be made to bloom earlier, as can magnolia, serviceberry, Manchu, pin and choke cherry. They bring birds to the garden, but arrangers who thought that berries from these trees might also enhance a design frequently find no more than empty stems after the early robins, grosbeaks, and cardinals are through. More reliable berries are the native and European high-bush cranberry, whose translucent crimson bunches glisten under caps of snow. Their sourness leaves them untouched and unblemished.

High-bush cranberry is also prized for its year-round reliability—even new growth will condition well—and has magnificent saucers of white flowers as well as berries. It is only one of a variety of handsome viburnums without which no garden is complete. They commence blooming in April (although Viburnum fragrans can be out in March) and continue to bloom through June.

Small white flowers are useful in mass arrangements. Deutzia and exochorda branches are solid with clear, white flowers in spring. The true bridal wreath, *Spiraea prunifolia,* has full stems of tiny double white flowers, each of them perfectly double and the right scale for miniature flower arrangements. Foliage for miniature designs is hard to find. Sometimes a few pine needles will be sufficient but two attractive shrubs with interesting, tiny leaves are worth considering. Stephanandra is low-growing with panicles of tiny white flowers. It is very hardy and will quickly cover a difficult bank. Sun-loving potentillas, both white and yellow, also have very small leaves, like miniature five-lobed palms.

Berries and coloured foliage add to the design of both garden and arrangement. The rowan tree (mountain ash) has red berries, which hold up very well in fall arrangements. They are also useful for keeping witches at bay, red being anathema to witches. In addition, flower arrangers seek unusual colours, and there is a mountain ash, which, while not easy to find, has coral-coloured berries.

Colours are at the top of a flower arranger's list, and colours in foliage in particular. Copper beech is a magnificent large tree with glistening plum-coloured leaves. For city gardens, purple-leaved sandcherry and weigela and the now-banned red barberry provide similar colours on a smaller scale.

Vines give the flower arranger berries plus line material that curves, twists, and tangles. Climbing hydrangea adds loose, papery edges to its bark, six-inch plates of white sterile flowers, and fuzzy fragrant blooms every June. It forces beautifully in spring with new buds showing green shiny tips against crumpled cinnamon bark. Clematis flowers are found in a myriad of colours and shapes. If the garden is large enough, the rapid grower bittersweet, with its brilliant fall orange berries, is a good addition. Convolutions of this vine are easily pruned and the tendrils are invaluable in miniatures. Speaking of orange, firethorn, when protected from northwest winds, will cover a wall with solid clusters of orange berries that last much of the winter.

In most arrangements, as in most gardens, flowers are the centrepieces. The framework of shrubs and foliage may well be attractive on its own, but the colours, subtle shadings, and various shapes and sizes of the flowers complete the design. For both the gardener and arranger the choice is infinite. In spring, for example, there are the always popular bulbs, narcissus, in its range of whites and yellows, and tulips of a thousand pigments and patterns. Arrangers are fascinated by the diversity of form in the flowers of the common garden tulip. They particularly like the curve-lipped petals of the newer green and white variety, Tulip Spring Green.

Less widely grown are small bulbs like the delicate iris reticulatas, the brilliant blue chionodoxa, and bell-like fritillaries, which are useful for small designs. Both ixiolirion with its cluster of lavender-blue flowers on 35-cm stems and Dutch iris with slender blooms of clear brilliant colours last well in arrangements. Later in the season acidanthera has small white flowers and a beautiful fragrance, and crocosmia flowers are an excitingly vivid red. Spectacular in tall designs and as exclamation points in the garden are the one-to-three-metre-high foxtail lilies.

Blue flowers bring bees and flower arrangers. One likes the nectar and the other the colour's ability to give variety and depth to a design. Omphalodes verna is a tiny blue spring flower that is ideal for miniatures. It is followed by blue perennial geraniums, perennial cornflowers, the tiny forget-me-not-like brunnera (perfect for miniatures), blue-violet alliums, blue columbine, and blue catnip, which is not very good for arrangements but is a lovely free-spreading blue. June and July bring prickly blue sea holly, lavender, salvias, blue perennial scabiosa, veronicas, monkshood, blue globe thistle and, the best of all blues, delphinium.

Daisy-like flowers have a fresh, open appeal. Doronicum is the first in spring. Then follows a long progression of daisies: shasta daisies, heliopsis, rudbeckia, small sunflowers and, for the birds or a very large design, giant sunflowers. Finally in late August and September the last of the garden daisies, the hardy asters appear, in white, pink, magenta, blue, mauve, and purple. Dahlias, which are a little fuller than daisies, come in gleaming colours and a fascinating variety of forms, from daisy-like to porcupine.

Tall, flowering spikes add another dimension. Astilbes' foamy stalks are all shades of pink to deep red. They may also be white, as are tall penstemon, creamy European meadowsweet and, in spite of its name, black snakeroot, which has long white panicles. For yellow spikes there are loosestrifes and the almost forgotten ligularia.

Saucers and open and closed cups offer still different shapes that make more solid areas of colour in flower and garden designs. Summer yarrows, often gold or lemon yellow but also pink, white, and red are good saucers. Spring's yellow trolliuses could be described as closed cups. Lilies are more open, campanulas are hanging cups; Oriental poppies and single peonies are giant cups; and Japanese anemones are delicate summer-to-fall saucers.

If blue is an important colour for arrangements, lime-green is equally so, giving light and excitement wherever it is placed. Lady's mantle blooms in June and July with a froth of lime-green and round, velvety leaves with good long stems. Several shrubs have lime- or yellow-green leaves. Golden philadelphus, euonymus, and privet each stand out in a garden, particularly on rainy days, and are beloved by arrangers for their colour.

Leaves, large and bold, are used in modern designs. Bergenias leaves are large and rounded and also well crinkled, so that their surface catches the light. A good variety of hosta is like pure gold in an arranger's garden. There are broad- and narrow-leaf hostas, as well as small leaf and variegated ones, and, with the variations in colour available today, some are gold. One large hosta with gold-green leaves is named Fragrant Gold.

Clumps of ornamental grasses vary the height line of a garden in summer and winter. They add both vertical and fountain-like qualities, as do the straight leaves of irises and falls of narrow day lily leaves. Grasses do the same for flower designs and add colour as well.

Most gardeners would consider a garden incomplete without annuals. Unlike shrubs and perennials, which have at most two to three weeks of glorious bloom, annuals' flowering is constant to the first heavy frost, as long as the dead flowers are removed. Annuals fill spaces left by spring bulbs and, in magnificent colour combinations, spill out of planters and window boxes. For the flower arranger, annuals mean not only the assurance of having flowers when needed, but also guarantee a wonderful variety of flower shapes and colours. Few arrangers would be without asters, marigolds, cosmos, zinnias, spikes of blue salvia, and another lime-green, bells of Ireland.

Finally, roses. What can be said about them other than they must be almost everyone's favourite? Almost every gardener and arranger has particular favourites too—florabundas, hybrid teas, grandifloras, miniatures, climbers, and shrub. With the excellent work of Canadian hybridizers there are roses now that will endure more of this country's winters than ever before.

For gardeners and flower arrangers alike, the delights of the garden are unending. However, so are the frustrations. There are so many marvellous varieties but never enough space. And while there are wonderful successes in design and in growing, there are failures too. Fortunately, there are always new beginnings…next spring.

CONDITIONING

Flowers and foliage are to the flower arranger what oils and water colours are to the painter and what clay is to the sculptor. For each, the quality and freshness of equipment is of prime importance. For the flower arranger it is absolute. One small wilted flower or leaf will ruin a design. As a result, maintaining freshness or "condition" in flowers and foliage has been the subject of study and research for years.

Arrangers generally agree on basic procedures, but many, through their own processes of trial and error, have found special solutions for certain specific plants that may or may not agree with remedies found by others. All agree, however, that the first requirement is to start with fresh flowers, either from the garden or the florist.

CONDITIONING
FLOWERS FROM
THE GARDEN

1. Take a pail of water to the garden. Always start with warm to hot water, except when cutting flowers from bulbs.

2. Cut flowers either in the early morning or early evening. *At both these times the plant has taken in water. In the evening the plant has also built up a good food supply. Never cut in a hot sun when much of the plant's moisture has transpired in its effort to keep cool.*

3. Make sharp diagonal cuts with a clean knife or secateurs. *A flat cut will allow the stem to sit flat on the bottom of the pail and possibly prevent water intake.*

4. Strip much of the foliage, especially leaves, that will be underwater.

5. Immerse the cutting immediately in water.

6. a. With soft-stemmed plants, take pail inside, preferably to a cool dark area. Make another cut underwater, 2–4 cm above the original cut. Keep in water as deeply as possible. *Water is slowly, but constantly being drawn up through the plant's stem by capillary action. When the end of the stem is exposed, air replaces the water and an air block can form in the stem preventing water from reaching the flower. Recutting underwater removes this danger.*
b. For hard-stemmed plants (chrysanthemums, roses, etc.), start with hot water, and slit up centre of stem 2–4 cm. Keep in cool water as deeply as possible.
c. For flowers with hollow stems (amaryllis, delphiniums, lupins, etc.), fill stem with water using a funnel or plastic syringe at the cut end.

Plug with a piece of cotton batting. Keep in cool water as deeply as possible.
d. For milky-stemmed flowers (euphorbia, poppies, hardy asters, etc.), sear and blacken cut end with a match or candle flame. Keep in cool water as deeply as possible. *The "milk" in these plant stems is a latex which, when exposed to air, dries quickly, sealing the cut end with an impermeable layer.*
e. For woody-stemmed flowers (lilacs, forsythia, etc.), slit up centre of stem from cut end 2–4 cm. Dip end in boiling water to prevent calluses from forming at the cut. Peel bark back 2–4 cm. Keep in water as deeply as possible.

7. Store pails of flowers in a cool dark area from 6 to 24 hours.

CONDITIONING FLORISTS' FLOWERS

1. Strip unnecessary leaves, especially those that will go underwater.

2. Place in water and make another cut underwater, 2–4 cm above the original cut. Follow the procedures listed above for the variety of stem. Keep in water as deeply as possible.

CONDITIONING FOLIAGE

Foliage improves immeasurably if it is immersed completely in cool water for a period of time before being kept upright with only the stems in water.

1. Large thick-leaved-plants like *hostas* and *bergenias* may be soaked overnight then kept with stems in water. These will keep 2–3 weeks, refrigerated in plastic bags. (This method does not apply to grey and hairy-leaved plants, which lose greyness when wet.)

2. *Broad-leaved evergreens* may be submerged for two to three hours then kept, with stems slit 2–4 cm up the centre, in cool water up to the first leafy branch.

3. *Deciduous branches* may be submerged for two to three hours. Their stems should be slit 2–4 cm and the bark peeled back to the same degree. They should then be kept in cool water up to the first leafy branch.

4. *Conifers* may be soaked in water up to one hour then kept, with stems slit 2–4 cm, in cool water up to the first needled branch.

5. Plants used to dry conditions, such as *aspidistras, ivies, sansevierias,* and *yuccas,* just need to be washed then kept in cool, shallow water.

To improve the keeping ability of flowers and foliage a commercial preservative is valuable. Lacking this, adding sugared, carbonated beverage (half beverage, half water) is useful. A small amount of washing bleach added to water helps to destroy bacteria.

SPECIFIC CONDITIONING METHODS

Below is a list of ten specific conditioning methods, the numbers of which may be matched to those beside the plant names in the list that follows it (except in the few instances where instructions are unique). In each case, instructions for *conditioning* are as set out in #1.

METHODS **1.** Condition—keep in tepid to cool water as deeply as possible for several hours or overnight. (Allow water to cool.)

1a. Prick stem just under flower head and condition.

2. Cut between nodes, then condition.

3. Sear stems and condition in 1/2 water and 1/2 any clear, sweet carbonated beverage.

4. Submerge, then condition.

5. Submerge, then refrigerate in a plastic bag.

6. Condition, fill stems with water, then condition again.

7. Dip in boiling water, then condition.

8. Split stems and sear, then condition.

9. Split stems, then condition.

10. Sear stems for several seconds, then condition.

PLANTS

Achillea, Yarrow − **1**
Aconitum, Monkshood − **10**
African violet, Saintpaulia − **10**
Agapanthus − **9**
Alchemilla vulgaris, Lady's mantle − **1**
Alstroemeria − **1**
Alyssum − **3**
Amaryllis − **6**
Anchusa − **7**
Anemone − **10**
Anthurium − **4**
Aster − **7**
Astilbe − **9**
Azalea − **8**
Baby's breath, Gypsophila − **2**
Balloon flower, Platycodon − **10**
Baptisia − **10**
Begonia, fibrous − **9**
Bells of Ireland, Molucella laevis − **9**
Bittersweet, Celastrusscandens − **1**
Bleeding Heart, Dicentra spectabilis − **8**
Broom, Cytisus − **7**
Cabbage, Brassica − **5**
Calendula − **7**
Calla lily − **1**
Canterbury bells, Campanula medium − **10**

Carnation, Dianthus − **2** (Keep away from apples, cedar, and chrysanthemums.)
Celosia − **10**
Chinese lantern, Physalis − **7**
Chincherinchee, Ornithogalum − **1**
Christmas rose, Helleborus niger − **1a** and **7**
Chrysanthemum − **7**
Clarkia − **7**
Clematis − **10**
Cleome − **9**
Columbine, Aquilegia − **10**
Coral bells, Heuchera sanguinea − **10**
Coreopsis − **1**
Cornflower, Centaurea − **10**
Cosmos − **1**
Cyclamen − **10**
Daffodil, Narcissus − split stem end, rinse with water to remove slimy sap, then condition
Dahlia − **10**
Delphinium − **6**
Doronicum − **10**
Echinops, Globe thistle − **9**
Erica, Heath − **1**
Evening Primrose, Oenothera − **10**
Fern − **10**
Forget-me-not, Myosotis − **7** or **10**
Foxglove, Digitalis − **10**

Freesia – *1*
Gaillardia – *10*
Gas Plant, Dictamnus – *1*
Geranium, pelargonium – needs nothing!
Gerbera – *10*
Geum – *7*
Gladiolus – *1*
Godetia – *1*
Grape hyacinth, Muscari – *1*
Heliotrope – *10*
Hermerocallis (day lily) – *1* (pick stem with
    many buds as flowers last just a day)
Hollyhock – *10*
Hosta – *4*
Hydrangea – *10*
Iris – *1a*
Ixia – *1*
Kniphofia tritoma – *9*
Larkspur, Delphinium ajacis – *1*
    (condition in warm water)
Lantana – *9*
Lavatera – *9*
Liatris – *10*
Lilac, Syringa – *8* (condition in hot water)
Lilies, Lilium – *7*
Love in a Mist, Nigella – *1*
Lupin, Lupinus – *7* and *6*
Lychnis viscaria – *1*
Lycoris – *9*
Lysimachia – *7*
Lythrum – *1*
Marigold, Tagetes – *1*
Marguerite, Anthemis tinctoria – *9*
Mertensia – *8*
Michaelmas Daisy, Aster – *10*
Mignonette – *1*
Milkweed, Asclepias – *10*
Monarda, Bergamot – *7*
Montbretia, Crocosmia – *1*
Mullein, Verbascum – *10*
Nasturtium – *1* (with warm water)
Nerine – *1*
Nicotiana – *1* (with warm water)
Pansy, Viola tricolor – *1*
Penstemon – *10*
Peony, Paeonia – *10*
Phlox – *9*

Physostegia – *7*
Poinsettia, Euphorbia pulcherrima – *10*
    (condition in hot water)
Poppy – *10*
Primula – *10*
Pyrethrum – *10*
Queen Anne's lace, Daucus carota – *7*
Ranunculus – *10*
Rhododendron – slit stems, *7*
    (boiling water for 5 minutes)
Rose, Rosa – *7*
Rudbeckia – *7*
Salpiglossis – *7*
Salvia – *7*
Scabiosa – *10*
Sidalcea – *1*
Snapdragon, Antirrhinum – *1*
Snowdrop – *1* (condition flower
    with bulb attached)
Statice – *1*
Star of Bethlehem, Ornithogalum – *1*
Stock, Mathiola – *1*
Strelitzia – *1*
Sunflower, Helianthus – *7*
Sweet Pea, Lathyrus odoratus – *7*
Sweet William – *2* and *7*
Tithonia – *10*
Trollius – *10*
Tulip – *1a*
Verbena – *1*
Wisteria – *8*
Zinnia – *7*

$\mathcal{F}$ORCING

Flower arrangers want the moon. They want forsythia flowers in January, delphinium in December, and a hundred other impossibilities in between. Unlike the White Queen, who believed in just six impossible things before breakfast, arrangers believe in innumerable seemingly impossible blooms before May! Many times they get them. Forcing is the secret.

Forcing spring flowering branches into blossom weeks ahead of their normal blooming time means speeding up the gradual warming process of spring, indoors. It can be done quite successfully with many shrubs, but it is not an exact science. Even with the most careful analysis of procedures and timing, branches vary in quality and time of blooming from one garden to another and from year to year. Good results in forcing depend on many factors including plant varieties, weather (everything depends on the weather), soil condition, stage of dormancy, geological location, and forcing procedures.

FORCING
PROCEDURES

- Cut branches on a mild day, especially during a thaw and, if possible, after rain because it helps the flow of sap. Noon, when the branches are full of sap, is a good time.

- Choose well-shaped branches with fat buds.

- Cut on a slant with secateurs or a very sharp knife.

- Bring branches indoors, split stems 4–6 cm vertically and peel the bark back 4–6 cm to facilitate the intake of water.

- Soak branches, covering them completely with lukewarm water, in a bath or laundry tub for 24 hours.

- Place branches in a deep pail of warm water in a slightly darkened, cool area (the basement, if possible) until buds open slightly.

- When buds show a hint of colour, bring them out to the light. The ideal temperature for this period of the forcing procedure is 23°C during the day and 12°C at night.

- To hasten forcing, add warm water several times a day and place near window but well away from cold glass. Spray branches each day with lukewarm water.

· To delay forcing put back in a cool dark area and add cool water.

· The nearer to their natural blooming time the branches are cut, the less time is required for forcing (see forsythia below).

APPROXIMATE
FORCING TIMES

Apple *Malus cvs.* Cut mid-march, forces 2–3 weeks

Birch *Betula spp.* Cut early February, forces 2–4 weeks

Bridal Wreath *Spiraea prunifolia,* cut mid-March, forces 4 weeks

Chinese Wisteria *Wisteria sinensis* Cut mid-March, forces 5 weeks

Cornelian Cherry *Cornus mas* Cut early February, forces 2–3 weeks

Downy Serviceberry *Amelanchier canadensis* Cut late January,
    forces 3–4 weeks

Deutzia *Deutzia spp.* Cut mid-March, forces 5–6 weeks

Father Hugo Rose *Rosa hugonis* Cut early April, forces 1 week

Flowering Currant *Ribes aureum* Cut early April, forces 1 week

Flowering Dogwood *Cornus florida* Cut mid-March, forces 2–4 weeks

Flowering Quince *Chaenomeles japonica spp.* Cut early February,
    forces 4–5 weeks

Forsythia *Forsythia x intermedia.* Cut January, forces 3 weeks;
    cut February—2 weeks; cut March—1 week

Hawthorn *Crataegus spp.* Cut mid-March, forces 2–3 weeks

Hydrangea, climbing *Hydrangea petiolaris* Cut mid-February,
    forces 2–3 weeks

Lilac *Syringa cvs.* Cut early March, forces 4–5 weeks

Magnolia *Magnolia cvs.* Cut early March, forces 4–5 weeks

Mock Orange *Philadelphus spp.* Cut early March, forces 3–4 weeks

Oak *Quercus spp.* Cut early March, forces 2–4 weeks

Redbud *Cercis canadensis* Cut early March, forces 2–3 weeks

Staghorn Sumac *Rhus typhina* Cut mid-March, forces 2 weeks

Witch Hazel *Hamamelis* 'Ruby Glow' Cut January, forces 1 week

$\mathcal{M}$ECHANICS

Flower arranging has a technical as well as a creative side. As in any specialty there is even a special language for describing the various pieces of equipment.

COMPONENTS are the parts of the design. This term includes *natural materials* (flowers, foliage, grasses, and ferns used in the design), *containers, accessories , bases,* and *mechanics.*

ACCESSORIES are objects sometimes used in a flower arrangement. They play subordinate roles, but a design incorporating an accessory appears to lack something if the accessory is removed. Accessories may be ornaments, functional objects, or organic materials such as shells or pieces of rock.

BASES are stands upon which a container may be placed. If used, a base is considered part of the overall design.

MECHANICS are the invisible components of the design. They are the tools that physically hold the design together. Arrangers through experience discover specific tools that are best for their methods and styles but will still have all the basics in their work basket. These include:

1. chicken wire
2. floral clay and stickum for anchoring pinholders
3. Mayfair cups: metal or plastic cups to fit on a bottle or tall narrow container
4. oasis: plastic foam, in many sizes, which absorbs water and is strong enough to support flowers
5. oasis cages: firm plastic mesh boxes to hold oasis in difficult positions
6. oasis iglu: rounded cages of oasis with a solid base
7. oasis tape
8. pincups: heavy metal cups containing a base of pin points
9. pinholders: small metal trays of pointed pins, in several shapes and sizes
10. oasis anchor pins: small plastic four-legged supports, which, when anchored to a container, hold oasis in place
11. tape: floral, green, and brown
12. wires: florist's green and spool of wire
13. water picks: plastic tubes which hold water
14. wooden picks for anchoring fruit, in two sizes
15. knives, flower cutters, secateurs, and wire cutters
16. sprayer for misting

$\mathcal{D}$ESIGN

A flower arrangement when completed is called a design. It evolves as the arranger integrates his or her imagination and creativity with the principles and elements of design. These are the tools of the mind in much the same way as "mechanics" are the tools of the hand.

Definitions of each element and principle as it relates to flower arranging may vary slightly from arranger to arranger and from floral art book to floral art book, but the essentials are constant.

DESIGN *is the arrangement of fresh and/or dried plant material and inorganic objects to produce an artistic unit.*

A designer uses the elements of design: space, line, form, colour, texture, and pattern in accordance with the accepted principles of art: balance, proportion, scale, rhythm, contrast, and dominance, to create beauty with expression, harmony, and distinction.*

ELEMENTS OF DESIGN

1. SPACE *is the open area around and within a design.* It includes the total space, which is three-dimensional, and the space or spaces planned within the design.

2. LINE *is the visual path along which the eye is led from one point of interest to another.* It is the foundation of all designs with plant material.*

3. FORM *is the total, three-dimensional effect produced by outline and contour.*

4. COLOUR is described as having:

    a. HUE, which is the specific name of the physical colour family (i.e., red, green, blue, etc.)

    b. CHROMA, which refers to the intensity of a colour and can be: *full chroma,* which is bright, intense and strong and describes pure hue, or *diluted chroma,* which is a diminished hue and is described as dull and weak. *Tone* is a colour not at full intensity. It is the result of adding grey or a complementary hue.

    c. VALUE is the lightness or darkness of colour. *Tint* is a light value of a colour; a blend of pure colour and white (e.g., pink is a light value, or a tint of red.) *Shade* is a dark value of a colour; a blend of pure colour and black (e.g., maroon is a dark value or a shade of red).

    d. Colours are also described as: advancing or warm (e.g., red to orange to yellow); receding or cool (e.g., green to blue to violet); or neutral (e.g., black, white, grey) which have no hue at all.*

5. TEXTURE *refers to the surface quality of materials.* Texture appeals to sight and touch and can be described as rough or smooth, coarse or fine, and glossy or dull.*

6. P A T T E R N *refers to the overall effect created by the various shapes, colours and spaces within the design and by the completed design (flowers, container, and accessories) within its own space.*

PRINCIPLES
OF DESIGN

1. B A L A N C E *is visual stability of an object when viewed from any angle or dimension.* A balanced design does not appear top-heavy, bottom-heavy, or lopsided. A design without actual or visual balance disturbs the viewer. Balance can be symmetrical or asymmetrical.

2. R H Y T H M *is the visual path through the design.** Areas of interest in the design lead the eye through and around the work. This "leading" is termed the "motion" of the design. It is accomplished by repetition, gradation, radiation, and the line of the design itself.

3. P R O P O R T I O N *is the relationship of the parts of the design to each other and to the whole.** It refers to quantities or amounts in comparison with one another (e.g., height in comparison to width, or height, width, and depth in comparison to each other and to the area occupied by the design).

4. S C A L E *is size relationship,** for instance, the size of one flower to another, the flower to the container, the container to the base, or the size of the whole design to the area it occupies. When variation of size is too great or too small, the components are said to be out of scale.

5. C O N T R A S T *is difference.* It is achieved by placing opposite or dissimilar elements together in a way that emphasizes difference (e.g., a rough texture emphasizes a smooth texture; black brings out the whiteness of white).*

6. D O M I N A N C E *is the force of one element.* It implies subordination and is achieved by emphasis of one element of a design, (e.g., repetition of shape, line, colour, or texture).

THREE MAIN
CATEGORIES
OF DESIGNS

1. T R A D I T I O N A L   O C C I D E N T A L includes flower arrangements in many styles, from Egyptian to European, early American, late Victorian, twentieth century, Art Nouveau, and Art Deco. This category includes mass, line, line-mass, Hogarth, crescent, triangle and geometric designs.

2. T R A D I T I O N A L   O R I E N T A L is a restrained art built around Oriental beliefs and practices.

3. C R E A T I V E is an art form using plant materials, generally with restraint. Creative designs include all those developed since traditional designs, such as modern, free style, and abstract.

REFERENCES

The Complete Flower Arranger, Amalie Adler Ascher
Encyclopedia of Judging and Exhibiting, Esther Veramae Hamél
New Dimensions in Floral Design, Marie S. Miller
Creative Flower Arrangment, Jean Taylor
Handbook for Flower Shows, National Council of State Garden Clubs

* *Horticultural judging standards,* Publication 34, Ontario Ministry of Agriculture and Food, pages 35 & 36.

GLOSSARY OF FLOWER ARRANGING DESIGN TERMS

TRADITIONAL   MASS a design of many flowers radiating from a central point
to form an oval, round, or triangular silhouette.
LINE a design with a well-defined line and a restrained use of flowers.
LINE-MASS a design with a well-defined line and a limited use of flowers
to strengthen the line.
HOGARTH a line or line-mass design that includes a Hogarth or "s" curve.
CRESCENT a line or line-mass design that includes a semi-circle.

CREATIVE   ABSTRACT a design in which plant materials are used as design elements
in unnatural and unusual ways. An abstract design may express ideas and
images or be strictly decorative.
FREE STYLE has no set pattern or form. The designer is free to select and
organize materials and is restricted only by the accepted principles of design.
INTERPRETIVE a creative design that expresses an idea,
a place, a thought, or an emotion, through the use of plant material.
MINIATURE a design measuring no more than 12.7 cm in any direction.
MODERN DESIGN a creative design characterized by bold forms,
sharp contrasts, and the restrained use of materials which are often grouped.
Modern design is constantly evolving.
PARALLEL a creative design of three or more vertical groupings in,
or appearing to be in, a single container with sufficient space between each
group to illustrate the parallel effect.
SMALL DESIGN a design measuring no more than 25.4 cm
in any direction.
SYNERGISTIC a design of three or more separate arrangements that have
similarities, usually in material and colours, and that are placed in sufficient
proximity to form one design.
UNDERWATER a design with some of the plant materials underwater
to give interest and special effects.
VEGETATIVE a design in which plant components appear to be arranged
in a naturalistic way, that is, resembling the way they grow.
WATER VIEWING a naturalistic line design, somewhat sparse,
in an open container with two-thirds of the surface area showing water.

PLANTS OF AN ARRANGER'S GARDEN: BOTANICAL GLOSSARY

TREES   EVERGREEN
Cedar *Thuja occidentalis*
False Cypress *Chamaecyparis pisifera* 'Filifera'
Hemlock *Tsuga canadensis*
Juniper *Juniperus cvs.*
Spruce *Picea glauca*
White Pine *Pinus strobus*
Yew *Taxus cvs.*

BROADLEAF EVERGREEN
Euonymus *Euonymus fortunei cultivated varieties*
Holly *Ilex x Meserveae* 'Blue Boy' and 'Blue Girl'
Oregon Holly *Mahonia aquifolium*

DECIDUOUS
Beech *Fagus spp.*
Birch *Betula papyrifera*
Corkscrew Willow *Salix matsudana* 'Tortuosa'
Fantail Willow *Salix sachalinensis* 'Sekka'
Horse-chestnut *Aesculus hippocastanum*
Maple *Acer spp.*
Oak *Quercus spp.*
Purple Beech *Fagus sylvatica* 'Purpurea'

SMALL TREES AND SHRUBS
Bridal Wreath *Spiraea prunifolia*
Cherry:
    Choke *Prunus virginiana*
    Manchu *P. tomentosa*
    Pin *P. pensylvanica*
    Purpleleaf Sandcherry *P. x cistena*
Crabapple *Malus cvs.*
Deutzia *Deutzia gracilis* 'Alba'
Dogwood:
    Red Osier *Cornus stolonifera*

Cornelian Cherry *C. mas*
Yellow twig *C. stolonifera* 'Flaviramea'
Forsythia *Forsythia x intermedia cvs.*
Magnolia *Magnolia x soulangiana*
Mock orange, golden *Philadelphus Coronarius* 'Aureas'
Pearlbush *Exochorda racemosa*
Potentilla *Potentilla fruticosa*
Privet, golden *Ligustrum vicaryi*
Quince *Chaenomeles japonica var.*
Pussy Willow *Salix discolor*
Rose *Rosa cv.*
Rowan (Mountain Ash):
   Coral berries *S. aucuparia* 'Rowancroft Pink Coral'
   Red berried *Sorbus aucuparia*
Serviceberry *Amelanchier canadensis*
Stephanandra *Stephanandra incisa* 'Crispa'
Viburnum:
   Fragrant *Viburnum Farreri*
   Highbush cranberry (European) *V. opulus*
   Highbush cranberry (native) *V. trilobum*
Weigela *Weigela florida* 'Foliis Purpuriis'
Witch hazel, Asian *Hamamelis x intermedia*
Witch hazel, Asian Red flower *H. x intermedia* 'Ruby glow'

VINES
Bittersweet *Celastrus scandens*
Clematis *Clematis spp. & cvs.*
Climbing Hydrangea *Hydrangea anomala petiolaris*
Firethorn *Pyracantha coccinea*

BULBS AND CORMS
Acidanthera *Gladiolus calianthus*
Crocosmia *Crocosmia masonorum*
Daffodil *Narcissus cvs.*
Dahlia *Dahlia cvs.*
Dutch Iris *Iris xiphium x I. filifolia*
Foxtail Lily *Eremurus spp.*
Fritillary *Fritillaria spp.*
Glory of the Snow *Chionodoxa spp.*
Iris reticulata *Iris reticulata cvs.*
Ixiolirion *Ixiolirion spp.*
Tulip *Tulipa gesnerana* 'Spring Green'

PERENNIALS
Astilbe *Astilbe cvs.*
Beardtongue *Penstemon spp.*
Bellflower *Campanula spp. & cvs.*
Bergenia *Bergenia spp.*
Black Snakeroot *Cimicifuga simplex* 'White Pearl'
Blue-eyed Mary *Omphalodes verna*

Brown-eyed Susan *Rudbeckia fulgida cvs.*
Brunnera *Brunnera macrophylla*
Catnip *Nepeta mussinii & N. grandiflora*
Columbine *Aquilegia spp. & cvs.*
Cranesbill *Geranium ibericum* 'Johnson's Blue'
Day Lily *Hemerocallis cvs.*
Delphinium *Delphinium cvs.*
Globe Flower *Trollius cvs.*
Globe Thistle *Echinops exaltatus*
Grasses
Heliopsis *Heliopsis scabra cvs.*
Hosta *Hosta spp. & cvs.*
Iris *Iris cvs.*
Japanese Anemone *Anemone x hybrida*
Lavender *Lavandula officinalis*
Lady's Mantle *Alchemilla vulgaris*
Leopard's Bane *Doronicum caucasicum*
Ligularia *L. dentata*
Lilies *Lilium cvs.*
Loosestrife (yellow) *Lysimachia ciliata & L.punctata*
Meadowsweet *Filipendula hexapetala*
Michaelmas Daisy *Aster (Hardy) cvs.*
Monkshood *Aconitum cvs.*
Oriental Poppy *Papaver orientale cvs.*
Peony *Paeonia lactiflora cvs.*
Perennial Cornflower *Centaurea montana*
Salvia *Salvia X superba cvs.*
Scabiosa *Scabiosa caucasica*
Sea-holly *Eryngium planum* 'Azureum'
Shasta Daisy *Chrysanthemum maximum cvs.*
Sunflowers *Helianthus spp.*
Veronica *Veronica longifolia & V.spicata*
Yarrow *Achillea spp. & cvs.*

ANNUALS Aster *Callistephus chinensis cvs.*
Bells of Ireland *Moluccella laevis*
Cosmos *Cosmos bipinnatus cvs.*
Marigold *Tagetes erecta and T. patula cvs.*
Salvia (blue) *Salvia farinacea*
Snapdragon *Antirrhinum majus cvs.*
Zinnia *Zinnia cvs.*

THE FLOWER ARRANGER'S LIBRARY

Flower arrangers use their books for technical information, for style reviews, historical or up-to-date, and for day-dreaming. A new book on flower arranging opens windows on hundreds of different aspects of a fascinating art.

The "new" book need not be a recent publication, however. Any book is new to a new reader, and many flower arranging books are classics, filled with information that will always be useful and stimulating.

The following list includes new books in print but also those excellent classics now found only in libraries, second hand bookstores, or arrangers' bookshelves.

BASIC FLOWER ARRANGING

The Complete Flower Arranger by Amalie Adler Ascher. Simon & Schuster, 1974. ISBN 0 671 21666 X.

The Complete Guide to Flower and Foliage Arrangement by Iris Webb. NAFAS, Doubleday. ISBN 0 385 15119 5.

Creative Flower Arrangement by Jean Taylor. Stanley Paul & Co. Ltd., London, 1980. ISBN 0 09 113631 8.

A Guide to Japanese Flower Arrangement by Norman Sparnon. Shufunotomo, Tokyo, 1970. Out of print.

Miniature Flower Arrangements and Plantings by Lois Wilson. Van Nostrand (Canada) Ltd., 1963. Out of Print.

FLOWER SHOWS

Encyclopedia of Judging and Exhibiting (5th ed.) by Esther Veramae Hamél. Ponderosa Publishers, 1982. ISBN 0 913162 01 9.

Handbook for Flower Shows. The National Council of State Garden Clubs, 1987.

HISTORY

The Art of Flower Arrangement by Beverley Nichols Collins. 1967. Out of Print.

A History of Flower Arranging by Julia S. Berral. Viking, 1968. Library of Congress card number 68 23997.

FLOWER
ARRANGING,
GENERAL

An American Style of Flower Arranging by Leonard Tharp. Taylor Publishing, Dallas, Texas, 1986. ISBN 0 87833 5374.

L'arte dei fiori in Italia. Leonardo-de Luca Editori, 1991. ISBN 88 7813 367 1.

Bouquets en France. Société Nationale d'Horticulture de France, 1990. ISBN 2 9502708 3 2.

Design with Plant Material by Marian Aaronson. Grower Books, 1972. Out of Print.

Fantasie Floreali, L'arte di decorare con i fiori by Anna Anzi. Giorgio Mondador & Associati Editori, 1991.

Flower Decoration by George W. Smith. Webb & Bower, 1988. ISBN 0 86350 181 8.

Flower Decoration in European Homes by Laurence Buffet-Challié. William Morrow & Company Inc., 1969. Library of Congress card number 7780900. Out of print.

The Flower Decorator by George W. Smith. Webb and Bower, London, 1988. ISBN 0863 50 1818.

Flowers in the Modern Manner by Marion Aaronson. Grower Books, London, 1978. ISBN 0901 361 54 2. National Association of Flower Arrangement Societies, London.

Flower Style by Kenneth Turner. Weidenfeld & Nicolson, N.Y., 1989. ISBN 1 55584 247 X.

Flowers with Style by Lena Malouf. Simon and Schuster, Australia, 1988. ISBN 0 7318 0002 8.

More Decorating with Flowers by Ronaldo Maia. Harry N. Abrams Inc. N.Y., 1991. ISBN 0 8109 3622 4.

New Dimensions in Floral Design by Marie S. Miller. Fisher Wegferd Publications, Oregon, 1981. ISBN 0 9606424 0 4. Out of print.

Practical Flower Arrangement by Jean Taylor. Hamlyn, London, 1973. ISBN 0 600 36992 7. Out of print.

Scultura Floreale by Paula Burger and Lori Marsano. Idea Books Edizioni Milano. ISBN 88 7017 055 1. (Flower Arranging Societies of Great Britain)

$\mathcal{I}$NDEX

$\mathcal{P}$ATRONS

Sponsors of The Canadian Flower Arranger made this book possible.
The Garden Clubs of Ontario and flower arrangers everywhere are grateful
for the donations from corporations, organizations and individuals which
has been so freely and generously given in support of art books such as this.

The Boland Foundation
The Roy C. Hill Charitable
 Foundation
The W. Garfield Weston
 Foundation
The Royal Bank of Canada
Eve's Flower Shop Ltd.
Mary's Flower Shop, Aurora
Matsu Garden Enterprises Inc.
Van Nes Flowers Limited
Aurora Horticultural Society
Markham Garden Society
Newmarket Horticultural Society
Peterborough Horticultural
 Society
The Garden Club of Ancaster
The Garden Club of Burlington
The Garden Club of Cambridge
The Garden Club of Dundas
Georgian Bay Garden Club
Garden Club of Hamilton
Hilltop Garden Club
Garden Club of Kitchener-
 Waterloo
Garden Club of London
Milne House Garden Club
Ottawa Garden Club
Garden Clubs of Ontario
Garden Club of Toronto
Toronto Japanese Garden Club
Eunice Denby Limited
Olga Alexander
Audrey M. Allman
Gay and Bill Anderson
Mavis Anderson
Lillian E. Arthur
Angela Atkinson
Mary Baillie
Anne Baker
Winnifred Barclay
Deborah A. Beatty
Sandra E. Beech
Aileen Benn
Ethel Benson

Betty T. Billes
Shirley and Gary Binns
Sadie H. Blain
Mary M. Bosley
Nancy Boxer
Agnes Brennan
Einar and Catharine Brevik
Jacqueline Brisby
Heather Brodeur
Dick and Theresa Brom
Marguerite Brooke
Barbara Brown
Elizabeth Bryce
Helen Bryson
Margaret E. Burritt
Reta Caldwell
Irene Christensen
Cynthia Clarkson
Marianne Cole
Elizabeth Coons
Judi Conacher
Anne Conlin
Dorothy Cottrelle
Edith Craig
Joan Creighton
Betty Crosby
Frances A. Culliton
Marion Dales
Patricia Dalton
Jennifer Deacon
Katherine Dembroski
Ann Diebel
Joyce Dossal
M. Downes
Miriam J. Drennan
Suzanne E. Drinkwater
Pamela Edwards
Margaret Elliott
Elizabeth Louise Ewans
Muriel Fairty
Jill Farrow
Marlo Finlayson
David and Martha Finklestein
Anna Finlayson

Muriel Flagler
Beverley Flint
Rachel Flood
Madelyn Foy
Joyce Frewer
Beth Frost
Heather Fuller
Dorothy Given
Joyce E. Girven
Alma Gomme
Anna Gwendolyn Gray
Flora Gunning
Marion Halliday
Maria Hanna
Mary Harding
Beverly Hargraft
Isabelle Heidrich
Mary Frances Hendrick
Anne Hertzberg
Barbara Hill
Julie and John Hillary
Grace E. Irvine
Shirley Irvine
Ella Irving
Robbie Isbister
Sally Jefferson
Helen Johnston
Ruth Jones
Ruth Keith
Mary Kernohan
Connie Kershaw
Leslie Laking
E. Aileen Lamont
Suzanne Law
Mildred LeGrow
Susan Lind
Marea Lyle
Ruth MacKneson
Doreen Martindale
Rose McBride
Katie May McCarthy
Brenda McCutcheon
Marion McIntyre
Gwen and Jack McKenna

Joan McMullen
Audrey Meiklejohn
June Miller
Gertrude Mitchell
Martha Mitchell
Elise Morrison
Jean Morrow
Margaret Murgatroyd
Elizabeth R. Nash
Maureen Naylor
Mary Nichols
Louise M. Nixon
Joan Pratt
Elizabeth Pigott
Beth Porter
Flavia Redelmeier
Joan Redfern
Jane E. Reeves
Irene E. Rickard
Ruth Ronson
Mable H. Shephard
Helen Skinner
Dorothea Smythe
Betty Somerville
Peg Spence
Joan Stevenson
G. Thomasson
Mildred Todd
Jeanie Turner
Mary van Straubenzee
Roberta Vaughan
Shelagh Watters
Dorothy Weir
Frances M. Weir
Dodie Wesley
Janice Whetham
Pearl Wilby
Anne D. Wilson
Charlotte Wilson
Mary Grace Wright
Eileen H. Young
Lois Young